EDITORIAL

Greetings everyone,

This Christmas comes with perfect timing for self-reflection, it's a great launching point to be reminded of the potential of the human spirit. This time of the year many are more giving than they might appear.

This holiday finds Pump it up Magazine traveling across the seas to the great country of South Korea. Our cover is graced with the talented South Korean genius RTMKNG (Rhythm King). Producer, DJ, songwriter and musician extraordinaire!

Our gift to you, is a winter wonderland of independent artists, fashion, South Korean beauty, and we top it off with our recommendations for the last day of the year, New Years Eve, and then we glide into the future ..the year 2020!

We hope you will enjoy this Christmas edition, and we wish you a MERRY CHRISTMAS and a HAPPY NEW YEAR!

Don't forget to tune-in to Pump It Up Magazine Radio to listen to your favorite artists both independent and major.

Anissa Boudjaoui
Founder
and Editor In Chief

CONTRIBUTORS

EDITOR IN CHIEF
Anissa Boudjaoui

MUSIC EDITOR
Michael B. Sutton

STYLE EDITOR
Grace Rose

FASHION
Krasimira Veselinova

PARTNERS

Editions L.A.
GRAPHIC DESIGN
www.editions-la.com

Your Music Consultant
yourmusicconsultant.com

Info Music
www.infomusic.fr

L.A. Unlimited
www.launlimitedinc.com

Pump it up Magazine

TABLE OF CONTENTS

⚡ **EDITORIAL** 5
Page 5

⚡ **MUSIC REVIEW** 10
How K-pop is opening doors for the Korean indie scene

⚡ **BEAUTY** 19
10 best reasons why Korean skincare products are better

⚡ **TOP TIPS** 26
How to promote your christmas song

⚡ **RTMKNG**
Multi-Talented South Korean Electronic and Pop Music Sensation!

⚡ **HAPPY HOLIDAY!**
- Christmas gifts for songwriters and musicians
- Our Christmas songs selection
- Top Indie Artists
- New Years's Eve in L.A.

⚡ **FASHION**
- The top must-have outfits for this new Christmas season

⚡ **CINEMA**
Best holiday movies to stream

⚡ **HUMANITARIAN AWARENESS**
How to give back this christmas

Pump it up
MAGAZINE

PUMP IT UP MAGAZINE

LINKS

WEBSITE
www.pumpitupmagazine.com

FACEBOOK
www.facebook.com/pumpitupmagazine

TWITTER
www.twitter.com/pumpitupmag

SOUNDCLOUD
www.soundcloud.com/pumpitupmagazine

INSTAGRAM
pumpitupmagazine

PINTEREST
www.pinterest.com/pumpitupmagazine

PUMP IT UP MAGAZINE
30721 Russell Ranch Road
Suite 140
Westlake Village,
California 91362
United States
www.pumpitupmagazine.com
info@pumpitupmagazine.com
Tel : (001) (877)841 – 7414 (toll free number)

RTMKNG

LIGHTS UP THE WORLD OF DANCE MUSIC WITH A NEW EP/MAXI-SINGLE TITLED

"Come Down"

Originally from South Korea, composer, producer, and musician extraordinaire RTMKNG lights up the world of dance music with a new ep/maxi-single titled Come Down . The project consists of a radio vocal version, a club remix, and acapella and an instrumental track. RTMKNG is an amazing producer whose sound is forever evolving and Come Down is another brick on the road of artistic validation.

Come Down opens with a radio version of the composition which features the vocal expertise of the talented singer Lumin. Come Down's driving beat and synth bass immediately captivate the attention of the listener. Lumin adds a soulful edge to the track's vibe. RTMKNG makes skillful use of the song's free space and contributes greatly to Come Down's vocal terrain for an exhilarating sonic adventure.

Come Down's "extended mix" keeps the party vibe flowing with an organic drum beat that sets the mood for this exotic groove to sweep you off of your feet while dancing to the rhythm. The track is further enhanced by its intricate use of voice samples and the elegant touch of Lumin's voice. Come Down keeps the listener's attention with its intense song structure, breaks, and drops. RTMKNG has certainly put together a masterpiece as Come Down is set to touch music lovers from all walks of life.

To Know more about RTMKNG, please read our exclusive interview
and visiit :
http://room24ent.com/

and follow @RTMKNGOFFICIAL on social media :

Download & Stream "COME DOWN" now on all digital platforms!

RTMKNG

1. GREAT TO HAVE YOU ON PUMP IT UP MAGAZINE. PLEASE, INTRODUCE YOURSELF.

Hello, I'm RTMKNG, an electronic dance musician in South Korea.
Of course, I do my music arrangements, play all the instruments, do mixing and mastering myself, but the most important thing is to create a catching melody. I'm pursuing music closer to pop than club music.
I love vintage gear and blues very much and I always play guitar on stage.
I have released my album with very talented Korean artists such as Ye-eun of Wonder girls, Bumkey, Hash Swan, Bonggu of GB9, and also wrote for Block -B, Evol, etc. as a K-pop producer.

2. HOW DID YOU GET STARTED IN THE MUSIC BUSINESS?

I have loved Blues and Jazz when I was 11 years old, and started playing the guitar. When I was 19 I became a professional Jazz guitarist.
In a word, I've been into the music business since I was 19.
In those days, I used to play the music of Joe Pass, Charlie Parker, Robben Ford, and Abert king. After the military band, I played a part in the backup session with famous K-pop singers and also made commercial music to earn money.
By chance, I submitted my demo to the John Lennon Songwriting Contest and the Billboard Songwriting Contest in 2009.
I won the electronics music section of the John Lennon Songwriting Contest Season 2 and Two songs got the participation prize at the Billboard Songwriting Contest!
Since then, I have gained confidence and been continuing to make K-pop and electronic music.

3. TELL US ABOUT YOUR NEW ALBUM "COME DOWN", AND WHAT'S THE STORY BEHIND IT?

The idea came after finishing a recent tour in Japan, I thought that it would be awesome to create a song in a chic mood!
That's why it's now bass- house style music.
Also, The choreography of the song has been made by the best choreographer in South Korea, Jaeyong Chung, Head of Dance Team, Wawa.
He has choreagraphed artists such as BoA and Girl's Day and has been a broadcast dancer with BTS, Big Bang, etc. I'm so satisfied that the choreography turned out really good. I am certain that it will catch everybody's fancy.

4. WHAT MAKES YOUR PRODUCTIONS UNIQUE? AND HOW WOULD YOU DESCRIBE IT? (GENRES/SUB-GENRES)?

I don't pursue a particular genre. I just express what I want to express.
I just think that music with *good melodies and hooked loops is good music.*
And since the root of my music is the Blues guitarist, I always try to show my root with vintage guitar sounds.
The guitar sound is my signature sound.

5. WHO ARE YOUR BIGGEST MUSICAL INFLUENCES? AND ANY PARTICULAR ARTIST/BAND YOU WOULD LIKE TO COLLABORATE WITH IN THE FUTURE?

I am strongly inspired by Daft Punk, Calvin Harris, Maxwell, Wah Wah Watson, Albert King, and Red Hot Chill Peppers.
I was not affected by EDM artists.
There's a song titled 'Can't take my eyes off you'.
I've created this song with Justin Bieber's voice in mind from the very beginning.
If I have a chance someday, I would like to record this song with him.
Also, I want is to make music with creative minds like me!

6. WHICH IS THE BEST MOMENT IN YOUR MUSICAL CAREER THAT YOU'RE MOST PROUD OF?

Singapore Music Metters 2012!!
At that time I only had an original piece titled 'Love Song'. Fortunately, I got the chance to have a 20 minute gig at "Music Matters".
For the performance, I composed, wrote and arranged six songs in one month and even performed with the band. Looking back, it was a miracle!
I think the songs I composed at that time reflects more of who I am and the music I'm about.
Also, many K-pop stars, including Exo's Baekhyun, Chanyeol, IOI's Choi Yu-Jeong, and Jihyo of Twice covered the songs I played at that time.
They were a great strength for me.

7. WHAT'S NEXT FOR YOU? ANY UPCOMING PROJECTS OR TOURS?

On November 26th, I will appear in a music show called SBS "The show" in Korea.
It was shot on a 5G multi-view multi-angle video including the stage of "Come Down". This video content was transmitted to live MTV Asia on SBS The Show(TV Show) in 18 countries, Myanmar Fortune TV live broadcast, Japan TBS recording broadcast, LG mobile application U + idol live, YouTube / Twitter The K-pop channel, Facebook / Instagram SBS MTV.
I'm making my own K-pop, where English-speaking artists and Korean artists sing in English and Korean. It has a completely different vibe from the existing k-pop and I'm going to go into the US market with my new music.

@RTMKNGOFFICIAL Instagram
@RTMKNGOFFICIAL
@RTMKNGOFFICIAL

HOW K-POP IS OPENING DOORS FOR THE KOREAN INDIE MUSIC SCENE

Korean pop music, or K-pop, is such an integral part of South Korean culture that the government has blared it through loudspeakers across the border with North Korea just to annoy Kim Jong Un. The music is a mix of genres, including pop, hip hop, and electronic, and mainly features glossy boy bands and girl groups whose labels strictly train them in dancing, singing, and comportment.

K-pop is also an economic boon for South Korea. Keith Howard, a professor at the University of London who has studied the genre, says that the country has seen a return of $5 for every $1 spent on K-pop—not only from the music, but from its role in selling other Korean products like Samsung phones and televisions. South Korean government agencies estimate that K-pop brought more than $11 billion to the economy in 2014.

It is 1992, and three young men in a boy band are performing in a live television talent contest. The sound is new: Korean lyrics, Euro pop, African American hip-hop and rap. They dance in sync. The studio audience goes wild. The judges in their prim suits are less impressed. They reveal their scorecards. The band gets the lowest mark of the night, and is voted off the show

The judges couldn't have got it more wrong.
In the next few days the song I Know climbs to the top of the charts, and stays there for a record-smashing 17 weeks. That night the group, Seo Taeji and Boys, ignites a revolution. Korean pop or K-pop was born.

Clever design and brilliant marketing. But there's more to a K-pop band. It's an expression of Korean culture, and the government has been more than happy to capitalise on its success.

K-pop is now a multi-billion-dollar industry. Bands like BTS and Blackpink are selling out in the US, UK and international stadiums within minutes and became the first female K-pop group to play at Coachella.
BTS is second only to Drake in international music sales.

The Korean indie scene is blossoming, and while you may think the success of K-pop could annoy its stars, it's actually opening up doors for all artists!

Those only familiar with K-pop may not know what to expect from an indie K-music showcase – there's not a smidge of a dance routine in sight. But the bands at the showcase put forward their own styles of indie, influenced by their Korean heritage

If you perceive "indie musicians" to be a group of music artists mixing and mastering random recordings, then you are wrong. Within the diversity of what Korean independent music can offer, it encompasses a mix of genres we usually encounter: from hard rock to electronic and jazz.

Indie bands are a much harder sell than K-pop bands, who can capitalise on their male/female fanbases and catchy beats. But the K-music genre is definitely something to keep an eye on.

There are so, so many good indie musicians in South Korea. The number of amazing musicians is growing !

If you would like to explore more of the Korean indie music, we created a special playlist just for you on Pump it up magazine Radio, everyday from 4pm to 5pm(PST)

www.pumpitupmagazine.com/radio
or
On Amazon Echo, just say "Alexa, play Pump it up Magazine Radio"

Enjoy The Sound Of
Pump it up

RADIO

Get the free Pump it up magazine Radio App on your smartphone or tablet, and you'll never miss your favourite music !

POP - ROCK - DANCE - RNB - JAZZ
Available on Google Play Store
www.PumpItUpMagazine.com

CHRISTMAS GIFTS FOR SONGWRITERS AND MUSICIANS

PRESONUS AUDIOBOX USB 96 STUDIO RECORDING PACKAGE

The PreSonus Audiobox USB 96 Studio Recording Package is the ultimate home recording package and a great music gift for the home producers, singer songwriters and musicians out there in need of high quality, reliable and above all – great sounding recordings.

This 2 in / 2 out USB 2.0 audio interface comes with a wide range of recording tools such as Studio One 3 Artist Software, as well as a whole host of plug-ins and samples from the Studio Magic Plug-Ins Suite so you're ready to record and mix straight away. You also get a PreSonus M7 Large Diaphragm Condenser Microphone, set of PreSonus HD7 Monitoring Headphones and XLR cable – just add your computer and an instrument and you're good to go! A great music gift perfect for anyone who wants to record at home or on the go.

BOOK :

126 Proven Techniques for Writing Songs That Sell is a must-read for anyone wanting to write songs and thus one of the best gifts for aspiring songwriters. She discloses 126 different melody and lyric writing techniques used by today's top songwriters.

AKAI LPK25 MINI USB KEYBOARD

If you have a loved one in your inner circle that is a budding music producer or EDM musician, the Akai LPK25 Mini USB Keyboard is a fantastic stocking filler and an extremely professional piece of kit that will be appreciated by the electronically inclined musician. Easy to use, budget friendly and extremely useful – a great music gift and stocking filler that won't break the bank.

FENDER MONTEREY 120W BLUETOOTH SPEAKER

Bluetooth speakers don't get any cooler than this! The Fender Monterey 120w Bluetooth Speaker has been engineered by the team at Fender to bring the classic Fender reliability, performance and sound to your home, apartment or student halls. You get 120 watts of power at your disposal thanks to a pristine quad-driver system (2 woofers, 2 tweeters) so your music sounds amazing at all levels. Connect via Bluetooth or the mini or RCA jacks for instant musical gratification.

HEADPHONE

The AKG K52 Studio Headphones are some of our favourite monitoring and mixing headphones on the market today, which have been voiced to provide accurate representation of what you're playing whilst recording. Whereas producers would normally advise against mixing music on headphones, these have been designed with 40mm drivers that deliver high sensitivity sounds for a powerful output, plus an extended frequency response so you can hear everything you're supposed to.

THE BLACKSTAR AMPLUG2 FLY GUITAR HEADPHONE AMP

Perfect stocking filler for guitarists. This nifty amplifier allows you to practice anywhere in complete silence. Simply plug the unit into your guitar, connect your headphones and you've got stadium-quality guitar sound straight to your ears. It's like having a Blackstar amp strapped to your ears!

NATIVE INSTRUMENTS MASCHINE MIKRO MK3

Widely used by electronic musicians from all genres, the Maschine Mikro MK3 provides responsive colour pads for instant beat triggering, sample triggering or synth sounds as well as a Dual-touch Smart Strip which allows you to slide your fingers to strum instruments, bend sounds, use Perform FX, and add dynamics to your sound. A great budget friendly beat maker for pro musicians that has been specifically designed as an easy to use, highly versatile option that beginners can get to grips with easily.

NUMARK PT01 TOURING USB TURNTABLE

As the Vinyl revival is in full swing, more and more people are enjoying the fact their favourite records are being re-released on this once inconvenient format. However, your vinyl collection doesn't have to suffer from the lack of portability anymore thanks to the likes of the Numark PT01 Touring USB Turntable.

A perfect music gift for the vinyl lovers out there.

Christmas Gifts Ideas!

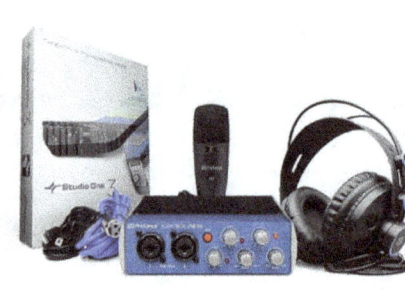

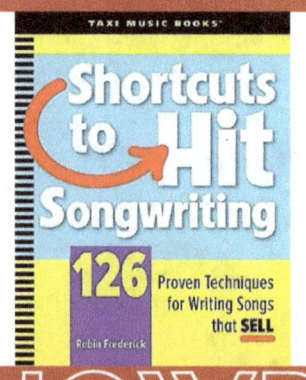

FOR SONGWRITERS & MUSICIANS

Your loved ones deserve a gift just as unique as their passion.

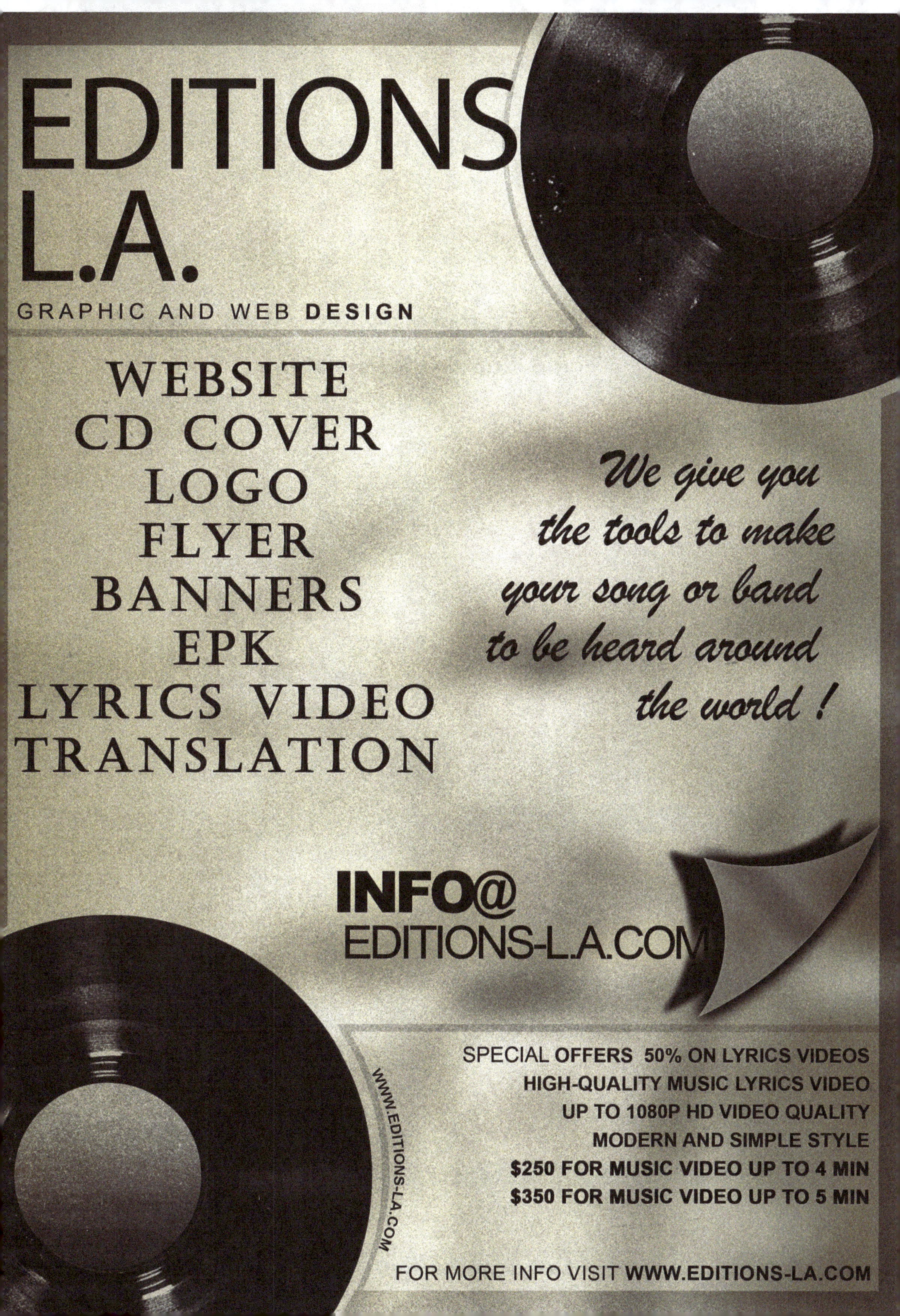

EDITIONS L.A.

GRAPHIC AND WEB **DESIGN**

WEBSITE
CD COVER
LOGO
FLYER
BANNERS
EPK
LYRICS VIDEO
TRANSLATION

We give you the tools to make your song or band to be heard around the world !

INFO@ EDITIONS-L.A.COM

WWW.EDITIONS-LA.COM

SPECIAL **OFFERS** 50% ON LYRICS VIDEOS
HIGH-QUALITY MUSIC LYRICS VIDEO
UP TO 1080P HD VIDEO QUALITY
MODERN AND SIMPLE STYLE
$250 FOR MUSIC VIDEO UP TO 4 MIN
$350 FOR MUSIC VIDEO UP TO 5 MIN

FOR MORE INFO VISIT WWW.EDITIONS-LA.COM

HAPPY HOLIDAYS!
CHRISTMAS SONGS

Our selection is sure to fill your heart with the joy of Christmas!
Playing everyday from 7pm to 9pm(PST)
on Pump it up magazine Radio

WWW.PUMPITUPMAGAZINE.COM/RADIO

JUEWETT BOSTICK - "SHADES OF BLU"

Originally from San Francisco, California, the legendary guitarist, singer, songwriter, and musical veteran extraordinaire JUEWETT BOSTICK has opened up a treasure chest of musical compositions upon the release of his new album Shades of Blu. Bostick is a musical veteran with over two decades in the game. He worked with the likes of the Temptations, Johnny Gill, Sister Sledge and a number of others.

Shades of Blu is Bostick's newest gift to the music world. The album is comprised of 17 selections, wherein we find Bostick drawing up life experience through the voice of guitar in a sea of life experiences. Bostick has cultivated a rare, but free-flowing melodic heaven that has appeal across the spectrum.

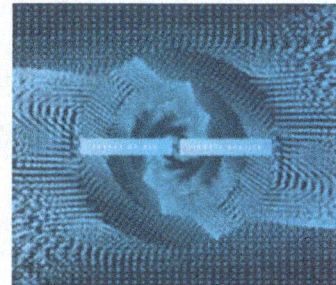

Shades of Blu by Juewett Bostick is a masterpiece that leaves the listener with a newfound cloak of inspiration and peace.
To know more about Juewett Bostick, please visit:
– httpps://www.nutbutton.com
– https://www.juewettbostick.com

MITCHELL COLEMAN JR. - GET FUNKY FEATURING FERNANDO HARKLESS AND ANEESSA

Funkmaster, Mitchell Coleman Jr.is gettin funky again along with saxophonist Fernando Harkless and smooth jazz vocalist Aneessa, Within the freedom of their own talent, they all come together to create a groovy, danceable tune that's excitingly delicious.
Another Michael B Sutton production, "Get Funky" is a funky mix with breathtaking tightness; the saxophone, electric guitars, flutes and the vocal cruising of Aneessa, all come together to make you feel that you are having a wonderful night out. Bonuses include inspiring piano and synths, and the formidable rhythm section of bass and drums urges you to burst a move or two.

"Get Funky" is just the kind of inspiration that modern instrumental jazz needs these days. More so to continue a relative rise among players who are finding ways for jazz to rise above the merely accomplished to become something that is emotional and compelling—and not just for aficionados but for listeners who might not listen to jazz as a habit.
No matter what situation you are in, "Get Funky" is a good therapeutic record to help you have a great time. Mitchell Coleman Jr's bass playing is at the foundation of this serious funk and there is one funky bass lick throughout " Get Funky" that makes one hope his thumbs are insured!
ton know more about Mitchell coleman Jr. , please visit : www.MitchellColemanJr.com

DRIVETIME

This time of the year, things are getting as festive as ever. While roaming the streets of New York City, I can see the lights and trees from shops and road installations, and even the music blaring from cafes and shops is getting really, really festive.

Many artists are join in the celebration of one of the most joyful periods of the year, and DRIVETIME is no exception. This talented act set out to create a charming, direct and unique Christmas release, aptly titled "Christmas Is Here".

The artist took the time to record 3 new songs to celebrate Christmas. The performances are extremely cheerful, with a nice production that highlights the upbeat rhythm and great musicianship behind this work.
To know more about Drivetime, please visit: www.drivetimeuoj.com

K-SYRAN

Merry Christmas (Where Are You) by K-Syran Norwegian singer, songwriter, and female rights activist K-Syran returns to the music world with her new single Merry Christmas (Where Are You). As a Billboard-charting artist, K-Syran is often praised for her inventiveness and unique style of voice. Merry Christmas (Where Are You) exemplifies K-Syran's stunning musicianship as she births a tasteful melodic gem filled with holiday cheer.

Merry Christmas (Where Are You) reveals another dimension of K-Syran's creative genius. The song opens with vocal charms from K-Syran over a ukulele strum and a light hint of harmonics.

As the percussion drops, a musical dialogue of a handsome bassline and guitar provide a warm backdrop to what turns out to be a spectacular folk-rock tune. K-Syran brings Merry Christmas (Where Are You) into the lands of perfection with a captivating vocal performance that is sweet enough to turn this groove into a mistletoe atop every household pine tree.

Merry Christmas (Where Are You) by K-Syran is a modern-day Christmas carol.

To know more about K-Syran, please visit:

http://www.K-Syran.com

TOP INDIE ARTISTS

ANEESSA - "SANTA BABY"

The beautiful pop singer and songwriter Aneessa draws attention from the music world once again with a special treat for the holiday season titled Santa Baby. Originally from France, Aneessa is able to graft a worldview on an American traditional song making this Christmas something that it ought to be - special.

Aneessa truly finds a way to reach the hearts of her audience and spread Christmas cheer with this lovely cover of Santa Baby. Aneessa is able to reinvent this lovely tune and make it her own **by also giving you a french version of "Santa Baby"** while maintaining the respect and honor of the original version.
Musically, Santa Baby by Aneessa is a holiday-picturesque composed by Michael B. Sutton, of backing harmonies, chimes, and a celebrative melody. Santa Baby by Aneessa is something special for this time of year!

To know more about Aneessa, pelase visit: www.aneessa.com

GROOVEXPRESS
"We wish you a Merry Christmas"

Jazz aficionados have made great headway in turning on listeners to challenging, cutting-edge jazz. Some tunes offer stronger impressions than others but even to more casual fans of the genre, a full blast of vintage instrumentation still offers that warm, nostalgic sound that feels lively.
Groovexpress, a collaborative music project, formed in 2010 by composer, arranger and producer, Mykeljon Winckel, know their music deserves and can net a wider audience than more traditional jazz records could reach. And they don't want to wait for the holidays to find you. On their single "We wish you a merry Christmas," Groovexpress plays loud and clear for everyone to hear and know what they are all about. After all, the holidays only happen once a year and it would be a shame to miss out on the festivities and the merry that comes with it.

Mykeljon leads a group of eight musicians playing multiple instruments such as saxophones, trumpets, bass, percussion, piano, guitars, drums and many more. That's a large group, and the inclusion of some instruments especially on a two-minute song might lead you to think the arrangement is needlessly crowded or exotic, but Groovexpress certainly make the different parts fit smartly within a larger compositional whole.
Let yourself be filled by that holiday spirit especially when it comes in the form of jazz music. It's complex, life-affirming music that's both serious and playful, steeped in tradition yet as highly original and forward-thinking as anything you're likely to hear this year.
To know more about GroovExpress, please visit: http://www.GroovExpress.me

ANGIE WHITNEY - "Mary Did You Know"

Times have changed so much, music has changed so much, but some records still sound pretty good with their warm nostalgic sound. "Mary Did You Know" is a Christmas Classic radiating from the deeply felt guitars and vocal performance of Angie Whitney.

But just as importantly, Angie's version boasts a breathtaking immediacy, which isn't surprising considering the strictly live-off-the-floor methodology with its carefully chosen instrumentation. The lively sound is stripped-back, not splashy, and there is no reliance on guest stars. Angie Whitney herself sounds incredibly focused and keeps things simple, far from slick but not dirty or messy on any level.

On "Mary Did You Know" there's also a high level of conviction that does not waver, and it's particularly impressive given that the song covers so many different settings of a religious gem. It's spiritual food for your soul. This is to say everything is set up to invite the singer's unforgettable voice. Your ear winds up begging to hear more of Angie's music. She has something special, and it's hard not to wish that this substantial talent had a more larger audience to experience her music.

To know more about Angie Whiney, please visit: www.AngieWhitney.com

DRIVETIME FEATURING JUSTIN GUARINI
"Love Has Found You"

Drivetime give themselves a hard task in making an entire song with saxophones, electric guitars and a piano, but still make it sound pretty easy. You have to be versatile and well-rehearsed with your instrument if you want to make an effortless song like this sound interesting.

Their holiday single "Love Has Found You" featuring Justin Guarini, the popular finalist from America Idol, summons thoughts of love or joy or some pleasant feeling that nudges you to start into a voyage of experiencing the Christmas holidays or as we like to call it, the most wonderful time of the year. At no other time during the year is the spirit of giving and sharing more alive in people's hearts.

For over four minutes, Drivetime and Justin allow you to just trust your ears, displaying rhythmic flair and the ability to produce inventive chords and making jazz music that is catchy and fun to hear while still offering serious pleasures in the originality of its composition and the verve of its improvisation. Nonetheless, you'll still be left in a mood of wishing you and others all the joys and happiness that comes with the holiday season.

Justin's unforgettable voice takes on the joy of brightening the minds and hearts of listeners. Although the holiday season is a time for all things red, green, merry, "Love Has Found You" also shows us that it's the time of the year where you celebrate and make memories with the people you care about most.

To know more about DRIVETIME, please visit: www.DRIVETIMEUOJ.com

PUMP IT UP MAGAZINE
WISHES YOU A
Happy NEW YEAR 2020

NEW YEAR'S EVE IN LOS ANGELES

Cheers to starting 2020 with fireworks, open bars, and dance floors and leaving 2019 in the rearview mirror, thanks to our guide to the best New Year's Eve events in Los Angeles

NEW YEAR'S EVE IN L.A

Los Angeles hosts some fabulous new years eve parties, from the glitz and glamour of Hollywood Boulevard, the crowds on the Universal CityWalk, the NYE Party in the Grand Park or the fireworks on the coast down at Long Beach and Marina del Rey there is something for everyone in the fantastic city.

There are many areas to choose from for your new eyar party with the greater LA metropolitan area being spread across such a wide area - iconic regions such as Santa Monica, Venice Beach, Beverly Hills and Universal Studios are all very popular new years eve venues, with a vast range of trendy clubs, bars, hotels and restuarants to choose from.

INSOMNIAC NEW YEAR COUNTDOWN

This year also sees the return once again of the Insomniac Countdown event at the NOS Events Center in nearby San Bernadino. This show takes place over 2 nights from 30-31 December and offers live music, pyrotechnics, costumes and confetti showers.

There's a top lineup once again this year, including The Chainsmokers, Alesso, Porter Robinson, Galantis, Oliver Heldens, Gryffin, Chris Lorenzo and 12th Planet.
You'd be surprised to know that the most sought-after makeup artist in Hollywood uses jelly petroleum on his celebrity clients. If you go to one of his masterclasses,

NEW YEARS EVE FIREWORKS

There are a few options for fireworks in the greater LA area on new years eve. The biggest organised displays are those at the Universal CityWalk new year party, on the coast at Marina del Rey and offshore at the Queen Mary in Long Beach, where you can also make the most of the evening with a fantastic onboard gala dinner and party.

For more details on the biggest fireworks displays in the LA area see our Long Beach page, or the family friendly fireworks event in Marina del Rey.

EVE AT UNIVERSAL CITYWALK

The EVE party on the city's famous Universal CityWalk at Universal Studios is one of the biggest organised parties in Los Angeles, and attracts huge crowds to an event taking place across a large indoor and outdoor area, with many of the Universal Studios most popular bars and restaurants participating.

This year the Universal CityWalk party includes a spectacular LED experience, 6 CityWalk clubs, unlimited gourmet food, a huge outdoor danced floor, midnight champagne toast, of course the fireworks displays. You can buy your tickets online here.

They also show on a big screen the Ball Drop from Times Square, which due to the time difference actually takes place at 9pm in California, a reminder of just how big this country is! We''' have the headline performers for this year as soon as they're announced.

KRISTIN CHENOWETH LIVE AT WALT DISNEY CONCERT HALL

There is always plenty of live music to keep you entertained in LA on new years eve, and one top show this year sees country music superstar Kristin Chenoweth performing live at the Walt Disney Concert Hall.

This promises to be a great show - you can secure your tickets via Kristin's official website here.

HAPPY HOLIDAYS

DECIDING WHICH PARTY YOU THINK WILL GET INTO YOU IS THE VERY FIRST MOVEMENT YOU SHOULD DO IF YOU DON'T WANT TO END IT UP IN REGRET. HERE ARE SOME BEST DESTINATIONS FOR NEW YEAR'S EVE IN LOS ANGELES!

Hilton Los Angeles (Universal City)

Exclusive time at the Sierra Ballroom, Hilton Los Angeles hotel, with a couple of fantastic performances from Davis (The Voice and American Idol), David Hernandez (American Idol) and Maya and Jake Simpson (The Voice Australia) will fulfill your energy to countdown and ring in 2020. Belinda Carlisle, The Go-Gos, will also make you all to dance and move your hips together before the champagne toast at midnight. The ticket price is ranged from $87-325 with Meet and Greet for the VIP ticket.

Grand Park Los Angeles (North Grand Ave.)

If you plan to take all your family members to head out, this place could be an awesome option. Since there's no age limitation and for take part in Downtown LA party, plus, the ticket for this LA's biggest NYE celebration is free. There will be three stages with various styles of music, LA's top DJs along with the local bands and or course the countdown at midnight with 3D digital mapping on city hall as the peak part of the party.

Union Station (North Alameda St.)

This venue offers you something different from other. When almost all venues show R&B or hip hop with the DJ, Union Station will show live Jazz where you can be swung elegantly. With DJs burlesque dancers, tray-passed oyster, and hard-roller cigars, people below 21 are not allowed to join. As the closing part, custom go-football will be dropped at midnight. However, there's no free ticket, since you'll be charged $150/person.

Pine Avenue Downtown Los Angeles (Long Beach)

The amazing street party along the Pine Avenue with numerous bands will be ready to get you dance with dozen bars which have been prepared to warm you. At midnight, you are going to watch the fireworks display from the waterfront. The tickets are sold online, with $30 only. The good thing is, it is not only for young people, but all ages are also allowed to enjoy the party.

When you have found where to bang the NYE, closing your day and relaxing your body in an amazing hotel will make your New Year even better. Here are some best hotels for New Year's Eve.

DoubleTree by Hilton Los Angeles Downtown

Located near the Grand Park, Downtown Los Angeles (0,8 miles) this 4-star hotel is highly recommended for you, Grand Park's party participants. You will feel its first-rate service with a warm choco chip cookie welcome.

Omni Los Angeles Hotel at California Plaza (South Olive St.)

It is a little bit difficult to find a great hotel when you visit Union Station. However, Omni Los Angeles is the closest 4-star hotel, with 1,5 miles from the Union Station. Luckily, its distance is close to the Sierra Ballroom as well which means you are free to choose between both hotels. As locating near the Hilton LA hotel, the nearby attraction of the hotel is similar.

The Westin Long Beach (East Ocean Boulevard, Long Beach)

Getting 9 minutes only (0,4 miles) heading from the Pine Avenue party to this 4-star hotel, make it super recommended as you wish the best waterfront view with incredible quality. The hotel grants you easy access to reach Aquarium of the Pacific in Long Beach, California due to its short distance, 0,8 miles only.

HOW TO PROMOTE YOUR CHRISTMAS SONG

Christmas songs are a lot of fun to record. You can put a new spin on an old classic, or write your own holiday-themed tune. Either way, it's a pretty good bet that fans will eat it up, especially because the holidays (and your holiday single) give you the chance to emphasize what your audience already loves about you: silliness, sadness, cynicism, whatever.

Then, of course, there's the discoverability factor. Music sales skyrocket during the last two months of the year. So many people are searching for Christmas songs during the holidays. If they dig your song, they might check out your other music too.

But there's a LOT of Christmas music out there. How do you get people to hear YOUR song?

1. GET YOUR SONG FEATURED IN A HOLIDAY PLAYLIST

Playlisting has become a huge part of how people find new music these days. And holiday playlists take things into overdrive, since the collection of songs can span genres and generations.

2. ADVERTISE ON FACEBOOK

With Facebook's targeted advertising tools, you can get your music in front of just the right listeners. And since the window for a holiday single is relatively short (just before Thanksgiving through late December), you can make a big impact promoting your posts for just a couple dollars a day.

3. MAKE A VIDEO — AND LET YOUR FANS USE THE SONG IN THEIR VIDEOS TOO

Facebook favors video when considering what content to display in your followers' feeds (as long as that video is housed on Facebook, as opposed to a YouTube link). So shoot a video or your holiday single! And post it on Facebook, YouTube, Vimeo, etc.

If you don't have a big production budget, you can create a simple Art Track video, or do a low-budget lip-sync video in your living room (maybe with a Christmas tree in the background and a fire in the fireplace).

4. GO LOCAL!

You might be overlooking a number of promotional opportunities right in your own backyard. Contact the local TV news programs, radio stations (especially community and college radio), and papers and weeklies. You might be able to get some coverage and radio play for you holiday music.

And if you partner with a local charity or non-profit (by donating a portion of the proceeds from your song), the launch of your Christmas single will be even more newsworthy. Plus you'll have the help of that organization when it comes to extra promotion.

5. BOOK A HOLIDAY TOUR (WITHOUT LEAVING TOWN)

Think about your favorite local or regional businesses, churches, restaurants, parks, tree-lighting ceremonies, skating rinks, or other public spaces, and see if any of them are interested in hosting a holiday party with music! Then make sure, once you get the gig, to use your holiday single and video as part of the online promotion.
Once you're at the gig, be sure to have CDs, download cards, and an email signup form ready to go.

Pump it up magazine

Aneessa

Beautiful Pop Rendition of the Eartha Kitt Classic

SANTA BABY

@ANEESSAMUSIC
WWW.ANEESSA.COM

FASHION

by Krasimira Veselinova

source: Pinterest

The fashion for this holiday winter season is very glamorous, with many solders in silver, blue, rose, white, black and gold. The party looks for the holidays are in many, many colors, just wear your favourite.
Yesssss, the winter is colored in the one of our favorite colors in red, blue, white and the sweet pink.

Choose also, the lather, but with many shine this is the new trend that you can see on the runway and wear on this holiday parties.

Be very glamour and in style for the new Christmas season with short fabulous party dress near your body.
You can buy one in white and gold or in blue and pink. The shine is the trend for this very special party look.
It's party time! So, don't miss the best must-have outfits with many shine, solders, silver and gold and the two nute colors for this winter in blue and pink.

Be inspired too to wear leather with solders and be with very diffrent party look.
The red is the special color for every Christmas season, this year wear the top trendy color on a party dress and with interesting jumpsuits.
This is the top three must-have party looks for this Christmas, the party dress in white and gold, the dress in nude blue in shine and the dress in pink with many solders.

MANY SHINE WITH SHORT PARTY DRESS IN WHITE AND GOLD

Short party dress with many shine in white and gold is the very special outfit for this holiday season. Wear with combination boots over the knee or very highheels with party bag in the same color.

PARTY DRESS IN NUTE BLUE SHINE

For this Christmas you can be in blue this is a very modern look, but definitely with shine. Wear it with shoes or boots and a little bag in the same color.

DRESS IN PINK WITH MANY SOLDERS

The pink dress with many solders is the look for this holiday, buy a very short dress in two pink color nute pink and in many dark pink color.

10 BEST REASONS WHY KOREAN SKINCARE IS BETTER

Korean products are the latest craze when it comes to skincare and makeup. There are so many reasons why these beauty and skincare products have captured our attention. If you trying to figure out what the hype is all about, look no further.

I am going to tell you all the benefits of using these innovative products and why you might want to add a few of them to your beauty arsenal. After reading the article I guarantee you will be scouring the web in search of Korean products.

1. SUPER CHEAP

Some people think they have to spend lots of money just to purchase a quality product. But when it comes to Korean beauty, most of the items are sold at cheap prices. Customers are able to stock up on Sheet masks, Lip Masks, toner and face creams without spending thousands of dollars.

If that's not a good enough reason as to why these products are better than others, then we have other points as well. Many people assume that these cheap items equate to cheaply made and low-quality products. But that's not the case at all. We did some digging to find out how the Korean beauty market has been able to offer products at a low price point that most people can afford.

2. NATURAL INGREDIENTS

There are strict regulations in some countries that prohibit certain ingredients in their skincare products. However , with Korean products almost anything goes.

This industry is big on using natural ingredients that are not typically found in other countries. The Koreans swear by their key components. The snail mucus has been used in cream and masks after the Koreans discovered the benefits. It's said this mucus helps to fade acne scar and hyper pigmentation while moisturizing and firming the skin.

The use of these relatively unknown ingredients makes the Korean products so much more appealing to people all over the world.

3. EMPHASIS ON BEAUTY

What really sets K- Beauty apart from other products is the emphasis on beauty. Korean women are taught from a very early age that beautiful skin is important, and they do whatever it takes to make sure they always look and feel their best.

To maintain their flawless looks, they don't just rely on applying a cleanser, toner and a moisturizing lotion before they go to bed. They go all out with a very intensive 10-step skincare routine

4. PERFECTLY MADE FOR YOU

Korean skincare products offer a variety of choices and it all starts with their cleansers. There are two types of cleansers available: Oil Based and Water Based. The Oil- Based ones are available in different textures, including creams, gel, and wipes. But that's not all, these products also come in various scents, from strawberry to cherry and warm vanilla. There are even unscented versions for those who have sensitive skin. With so many options customers are able to find the exact texture and scent they desire. And again, they don't have to spend a ton of money to get these hands-on items that are perfectly made for them.

10 BEST REASONS WHY KOREAN SKINCARE IS BETTER

5. INNOVATIVE

Korean products have completely changed the skincare and makeup industry. Because they are always developing new and exciting products, other companies across the globe are struggling to keep up with them.
We have seen many innovative products that have been developed in Korea. But one of the most popular is cushion foundation. This ingenious product was first introduced in Korea back in 2011.
It became insanely popular because it was easy to apply, and also it included the Korean's favorite component SPF. Essentially, a cushion Foundation is a liquid-based- formula that's stored in a compact instead of a bottle. These foundations provide light to medium coverage and hydrate the skin while providing an illuminating effect.

6. NOT A HASSLE

When we mentioned that the Koreans like to keep their skin looking amazing by using a 10-step skincare routine, I am sure you probably cringed. Well, Korean products are designed to make you look forward to using them day after day. Cool packaging, high -quality materials, and great prices are just a few of the benefits of these products. Korean companies create products that are very appealing in so many different ways. Just take this clay mask, for example, when it comes in contact with the air, the mask forms tiny little bubbles all over your face.

7. SELF-LOVE

Any product that promotes self-love deserves the attention that they receive. In some areas of the world, many people see skincare as a chore. But this is not the case with Korean women. They are committed to their beauty regimen, they see it as a way to provide their mind and bodies with so much care and love.

8. FUN AND PLAYFUL

Korean Skincare products are best because they are so much fun to use. If you search through social media, you are bound to find a bunch of beauty lovers using these playful and wacky products.
But they are not the only one who is having fun with their k-beauty items even celebrities are getting in on the action too.

9. ALL ABOUT PREVENTION

Many brands promise to get rid of wrinkles, restore damaged skin, and rewind the hands of time.
There are a lot of Korean beauty products that claim to do the same, too. They are able to fight skin issues just as well if not better than other products on the market.
But the K- beauty industry is really focused on prevention. This means, Koreans don't wait until a pesky skin problem occurs, they start using products at a very early age.

10. TECH-DRIVEN

When you think of Beauty products, the word "Technology" probably isn't the first thing that comes to mind. This is one of the main reasons why k-beauty products are better than the rest.
The Korean culture is tied to technological advancements, and companies work around the clock to create new products. To help drive the market, Korean skincare customers have taken to their social media accounts to help shape the entire market.
The website PEACH&LILY is focused on exploring all the hidden wonders of the Korean skincare industry. This informative website also provides tips and tricks on how to get the best use out of the products, and a marketplace to buy items.

BEST HOLIDAY MOVIES TO STREAM

With the abundance of streaming platforms at our disposal these days there are plenty of Christmas classics to put on. We rounded up the best Christmas movies !

A CHRISTMAS PRINCE: THE ROYAL BABY: DECEMBER 5

Now, the Christmas movie you've been waiting for since last year! In the third installment of A Christmas Prince, Queen Amber Moore (Rose McIver) and King Richard (Ben Lamb) are expecting a child. Of course, you can't have a movie about bb royalty without an "ancient curse"! Haven't you seen Sleeping Beauty, Tangled, or Ella Enchanted? I'm scared.

LET IT SNOW

Multiple storylines of teens dealing with relationships, friends, and friends who maybe want to be more than friends come together during one fateful Christmas Eve snowstorm in Let It Snow. (Think Love Actually but with more waffles and more Kiernan Shipka.)

It's based on the novel comprised of three short stories that intersect by YA masters John Green, Maureen Johnson, and Lauren Myracle, so you can expect some seriously heartwarming and funny moments. Since its release on Nov. 8th, Let It Snow is already taking Twitter by storm with viewers praising its sweetest scenes, as well as its positive representation of LGBTQ+ relationships and family dynamics.

HOLIDAY RUSH

Popular radio DJ Rush Williams and his four kids, who are used to living a lavish lifestyle, get a heavy dose of reality when Rush loses his job right before the holidays.

But when the radio station where Rush had his first job conveniently comes up for sale, not all the family's holiday cheer is lost. With some help from his producer and his aunt (Marlene Love), plus a healthy dose of the simpler life with his family, Rush just might be able to put his plans for Christmas back on the air.

THE KNIGHT BEFORE CHRISTMAS

The Knight Before Christmas officially gets the award for the best Christmas pun/title on this list. Vanessa Hudgens stars as Brooke, a teacher who has given up on love until she (quite literally) runs into Sir Cole Christopher Frederick Lyons, a medieval knight who has somehow ended up in the present day. Brooke, of course, feels compelled to help Sir Cole get back to his right time period or remember who he actually is—whichever comes first. That is, unless Brooke and Sir Cole find themselves living happily ever after instead..

CHRISTMAS WITH A VIEW

Vivica A. Fox and Patrick Duffy star in this Christmas rom-com, which tells the story of an aspiring restaurant owner who meets a famous chef when he comes to work at her hotel. As you might guess, things get ~spicy~ from there.

THE CHRISTMAS CHRONICLES

Kurt Russell stars as a cool-as-hell Santa (obviously) who gets stuck after two kids steal away in his sleigh (landing them on the naughty list, for sure). Come for Kurt, stay for the hilarious dialogue.

YOUR MUSIC CONSULTANT

"YOU BELIEVE, SO DO WE!"

We Can Help You To Grow Your Business

We are a monthly based service, we put faith in artists who has major potential, believed in them, and who are willing to spend their time and own money to work with us in building a successful music career!

Digital Marketing Services

SOCIAL MEDIA - STREAMING SERVICES - MUSIC DISTRIBUTION - PRESS RELEASE - PRESS DISTRIBUTION - PR

Radio Airplay and TV Commercial

TERRESTRIAL AND DIGITAL RADIO CAMPAIGN AL GENRES EXCEPT HEAVY METAL -
CABLE TV AND MAJOR NETWORK COMMERCIAL

Licensing & Booking

CONCERTS, LIVE MUSIC, EVENTS, CLUB NIGHTS - RED CARPETS -
FOREIGN LICENSING AND SUBOPUBLISHING

Why Choose Us ?

3 DECADES OF MUSIC BUSINESS EXPERIENCE
Platinum and Gold Records
MOTOWN RECORDS
UNIVERSAL
SONY
CAPITOL RECORDS

WE WORKED WITH:
Kanye West - Jay Z - Stevie Wonder - Michael Jackson - Germaine Jackson - Smokey Robinson - Dionne Warwick - Cheryl Lynn - The Originals -

📞 **1-818-514-0038**
(Ext. 1)
Monday - Friday / 9am to 6pm

FIND US :

www.YourMusicConsultant.com
30721 Russell Ranch Road Suite 140 Westlake Village, USA
Email : info@yourmusicconsultant.com

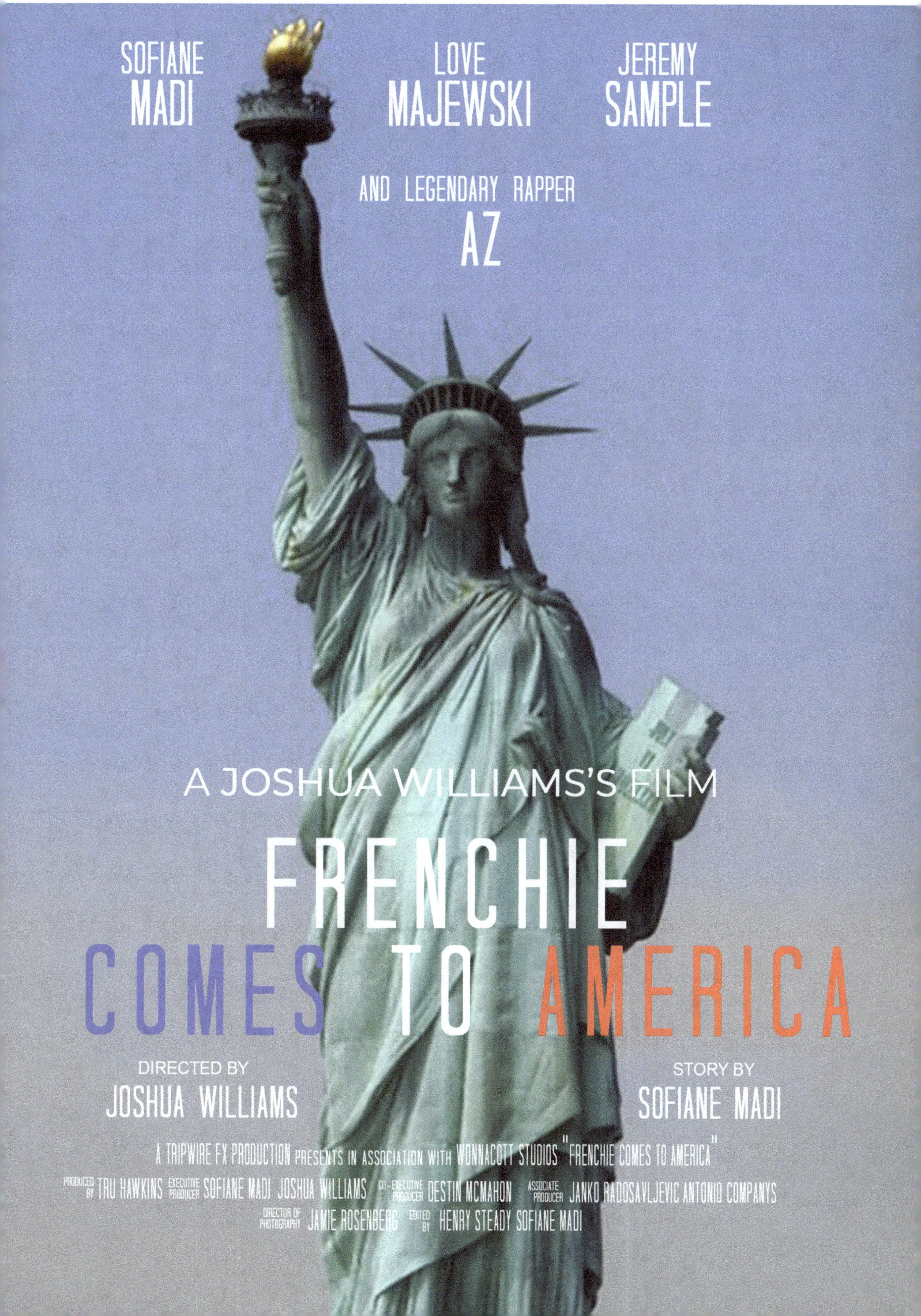

SOFIANE
MADI

LOVE
MAJEWSKI

JEREMY
SAMPLE

AND LEGENDARY RAPPER
AZ

A JOSHUA WILLIAMS'S FILM

FRENCHIE COMES TO AMERICA

DIRECTED BY
JOSHUA WILLIAMS

STORY BY
SOFIANE MADI

A TRIPWIRE FX PRODUCTION PRESENTS IN ASSOCIATION WITH WONNACOTT STUDIOS "FRENCHIE COMES TO AMERICA"
PRODUCED BY TRU HAWKINS EXECUTIVE PRODUCER SOFIANE MADI JOSHUA WILLIAMS CO-EXECUTIVE PRODUCER DESTIN MCMAHON ASSOCIATE PRODUCER JANKO RADOSAVLJEVIC ANTONIO COMPANYS
DIRECTOR OF PHOTOGRAPHY JAMIE ROSENBERG EDITED BY HENRY STEADY SOFIANE MADI

HOW TO GIVE BACK THIS CHRISTMAS

There are hundreds of ways to give back over the Christmas season but we thought we'd make it easy for you and list a few ideas!

Pick one thing and do it this Christmas season. God will love you all the more for it.

SPEND TIME WITH THE ELDERLY

Especially those who are homebound or in assisted living. Help an elderly neighbor with Christmas decorations, grocery shopping, yard maintenance -- or simply spend some time with them talking and being a companion. This will mean more to them than you will ever know.
Make time for your kids to see their grandparents — or at least talk on the phone — and learn more about their history. Recording or writing down stories of the past are gifts you and your family will treasure in the years to come.

FEEDING AMERICA

The Feeding America nationwide network of food banks secures and distributes 4.3 billion meals each year through food pantries and meal programs throughout the United States and leads the nation to engage in the fight against hunger. Contact your local community food bank to find food or click here to read about public assistance programs.

PUT TOGETHER A BOX FOR SOLDIERS OVERSEAS.

They need/want things that we take for granted. Shampoo, baby wipes, hand sanitizer, sunscreen, magazines, towels, Christmas decorations, candy, bottled water, tylenol, books, tampons/pads, lotion, chap stick, deodorant, phone cards, baked goods, beanie babies to give to children, the list goes on!

HELP YOUR NEIGHBOURS

Whether it's the elderly couple whose driveway needs shoveling or the single mom who could use a mother's helper, you probably have someone on your own block who could use a hand. Your family may be able to offer the lifeline they need during the holiday season.

MAKE PERSONAL HYGIENE CHRISTMAS STOCKINGS FOR A LOCAL HOMELESS SHELTER.

Personal hygiene items can be bought in bulk fairly cheaply. Throw in some candy and hats, scarves or mittens with a hand-written note. A good project for the entire family.

The most precious gift you can offer the needy this time of year is your time. Volunteers are always needed and appreciated during the holiday season. Take a few hours out of your week and donate your time to local shelter programs, soup kitchens or other organizations that are overwhelmed with requests for assistance this time of year.

TOYS FOR TOTS

Take your family to shop for a less fortunate child and teach your children invaluable lessons on thankfulness, empathy, and charitable giving. Purchase a new toy and take it (unwrapped) to a U.S. Marines' Toys for Tots drop-off location between October and December.

www.ingramcontent.com/pod-product-compliance
Lightning Source LLC
Chambersburg PA
CBHW080902010526
44118CB00015B/2234